The Clue Books

BIRDS

GWEN ALLEN
JOAN DENSLOW

illustrations by
E. A. R. ENNION

OXFORD UNIVERSITY PRESS

Oxford University Press, Walton Street, Oxford OX2 6DP

OXFORD LONDON
NEW YORK TORONTO MELBOURNE AUCKLAND
KUALA LUMPUR SINGAPORE HONG KONG TOKYO
DELHI BOMBAY CALCUTTA MADRAS KARACHI
NAIROBI DAR ES SALAAM CAPE TOWN

and associated companies in
BEIRUT BERLIN IBADAN MEXICO CITY NICOSIA

Oxford is a trade mark of Oxford University Press

FIRST PUBLISHED 1968
REPRINTED (WITH CORRECTIONS) 1970, 1973, 1976, 1979, 1981, 1982, 1984

PRINTED IN CHINA BY BRIGHT SUN (SHENZHEN) PRINTING LTD.

Birds of many different kinds may be seen in gardens, parks, woods and fields, by rivers and lakes and near the sea.

Birds can be attracted to gardens by putting out a variety of foods. It is best to put food on a bird table; here the birds are safe from cats.

You may like to make a table like the one in the picture on page 4, or a simpler one made from a flat piece of wood or an old tray nailed to a post.

Put out cheese rinds, seeds, berries, apple slices, bacon rind and bread. Hang nuts or scraps of food in a wire container or net nylon bag. Put fat in an empty coconut shell or hang suet from a string. If you have no bird table, all these containers can be hung from branches or posts.

A dish of water is very important.

The clues on pages 10–22 will help you to name the birds that come to the table.

Birds do not all behave in the same way. Each kind has its own pattern of behaviour.

Watch them carefully and record in a book what you have seen.

A book like this is called a FIELD NOTEBOOK.

Keep records like this:—

Give each type of bird a different page.

At the top of the page write a description of the bird (see page 7) and stick in a picture of it (if you can find one).

Then draw six columns and give them headings like this:

date	time of day	kind of weather	what the bird ate	what the bird did	was the bird alone?

Every time you see a bird at your table record it in your book.

When you have been using your book for a few weeks, you will be able to answer questions like these:

How many different kinds of bird visited the table?
Which kind of bird visited the table most often?

and for each kind of bird:

In what sort of weather did it come most often?

At what time of day did it come most often?

Did it prefer any particular type of food?

Did it chase other birds away or threaten them, and if so how?

Was it usually alone or with other birds of the same kind?

threat displays

Try to think of other questions to answer about the birds that visit your table.

Look for birds wherever you are, on a walk in the country, by a river or lake, by the sea, in your garden, in the park or at the zoo.

Write down in your field notebook descriptions of the birds you see and where you see them. You may not be able to see these birds as clearly as in the illustrations in this book, but try to make notes about:

the size of each bird
the shape of its body (See pages 18–22)
the shape of its beak (See pages 11–13)
the kind of feet and legs it has (See pages 14 and 15)
its colour
how it walks, hops or flies
what it is doing
how it behaves with other birds

The parts of the bird named in the illustration on page 8 will help you to make records of the position of the various coloured parts.

Look for footprints in mud, sand and snow. (See pages 16 and 17)

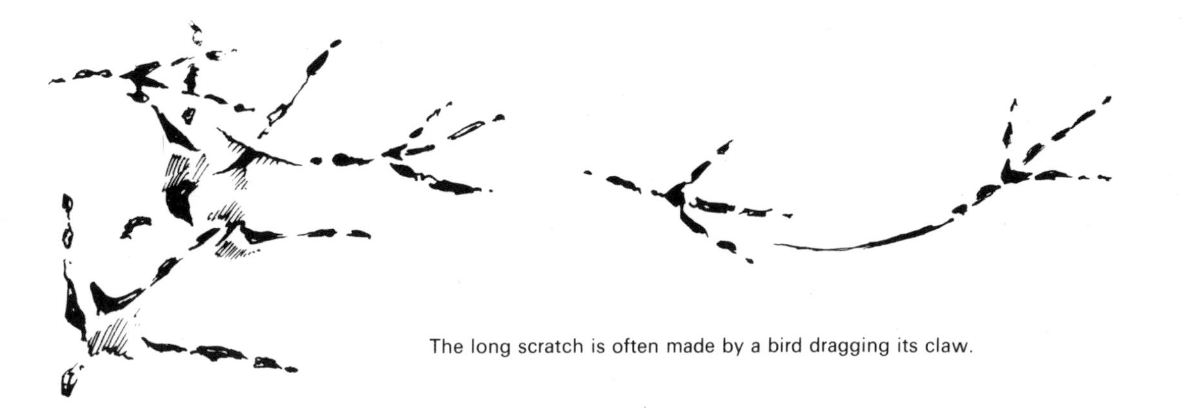

The long scratch is often made by a bird dragging its claw.

A drawing to show the parts of a bird.

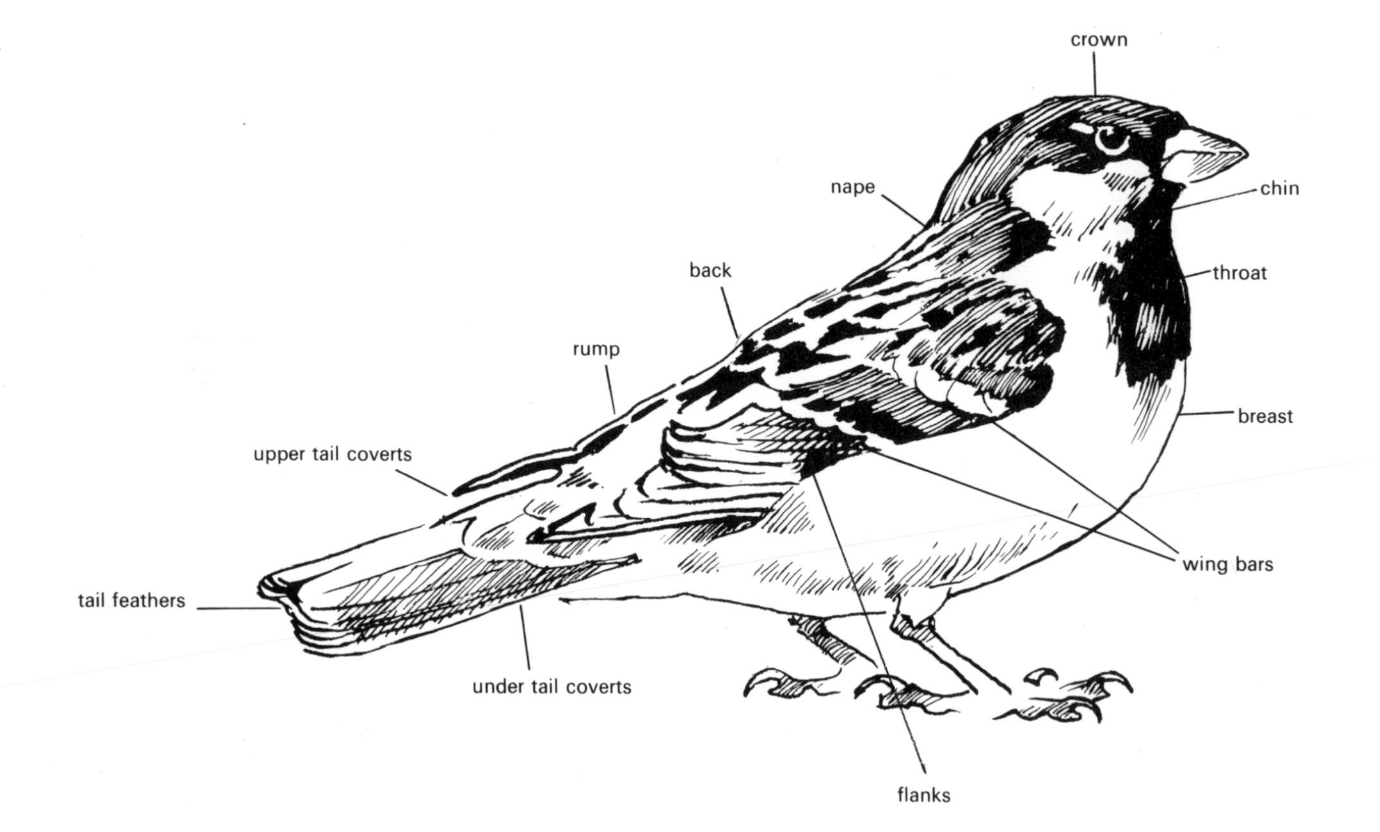

The feathers of a bird are called its plumage.

Every year, usually in the autumn, a bird loses some of its feathers. This is called moulting.

Collect feathers and mount them on stiff paper. Put together the feathers that look alike. When you have learned to recognise a lot of birds, see if you can decide which feathers come from which kind of bird.

Some feathers change colour when you look at them from different angles. Feathers like this are called iridescent.

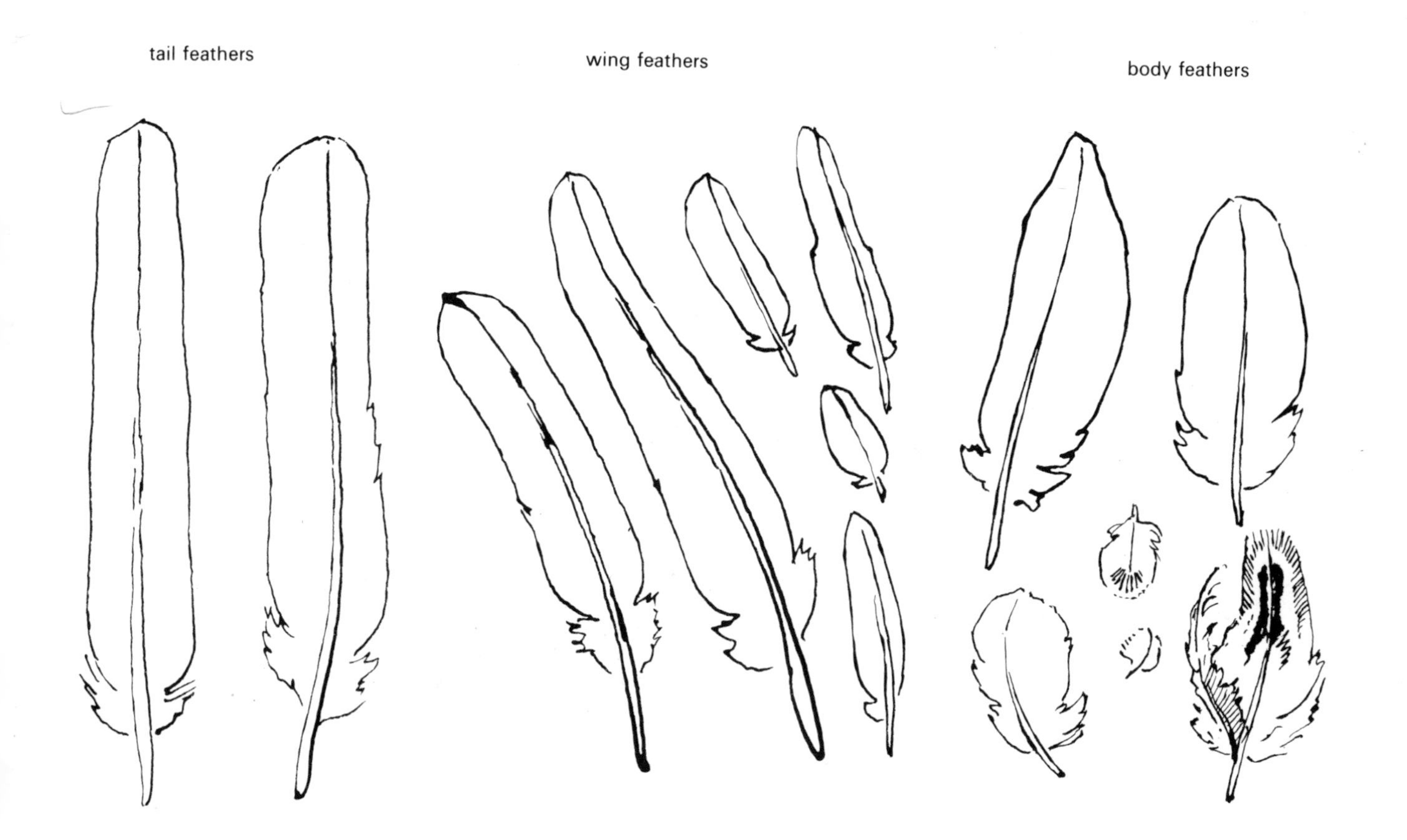

SIZE and SHAPE

If the bird is less than 30 cm long (a house sparrow is half this length, see page 8)	turn to page 11
If the bird is more than 30 cm long and is seen on or near water	turn to page 12
If the bird is more than 30 cm long and seen away from water	turn to page 13

FEET and LEGS

If the foot has no web between the toes	turn to page 14
If the foot is webbed	turn to page 15

FOOTPRINTS

If you have found footprints	turn to page 16

SHAPES and MOVEMENT

If you have been watching birds moving	turn to pages 18–22
If you have watched birds flying	turn to pages 18, 19
If you have watched birds on the ground	turn to page 20
If you have watched birds in trees	turn to page 21
If you have watched birds swimming	turn to page 22

SMALL BIRDS of sparrow size (15 cm or less)

If the bird has a stumpy beak — turn to pages 24–26

If it has a small beak and often hangs upside down — turn to pages 32–33

If it has a short slender beak — turn to pages 27, 30, 31, 33

If it has a forked tail and a quick wheeling flight — turn to pages 34–35

SMALL BIRDS of blackbird size (20 cm to 25 cm)

If it has a slender beak — turn to pages 28–29
if seen on the sea
turn to page 44

If it has a long, strong beak — turn to page 36

If it has a hooked beak — turn to page 40

LARGE BIRDS more than 30 cm long

Usually seen near water

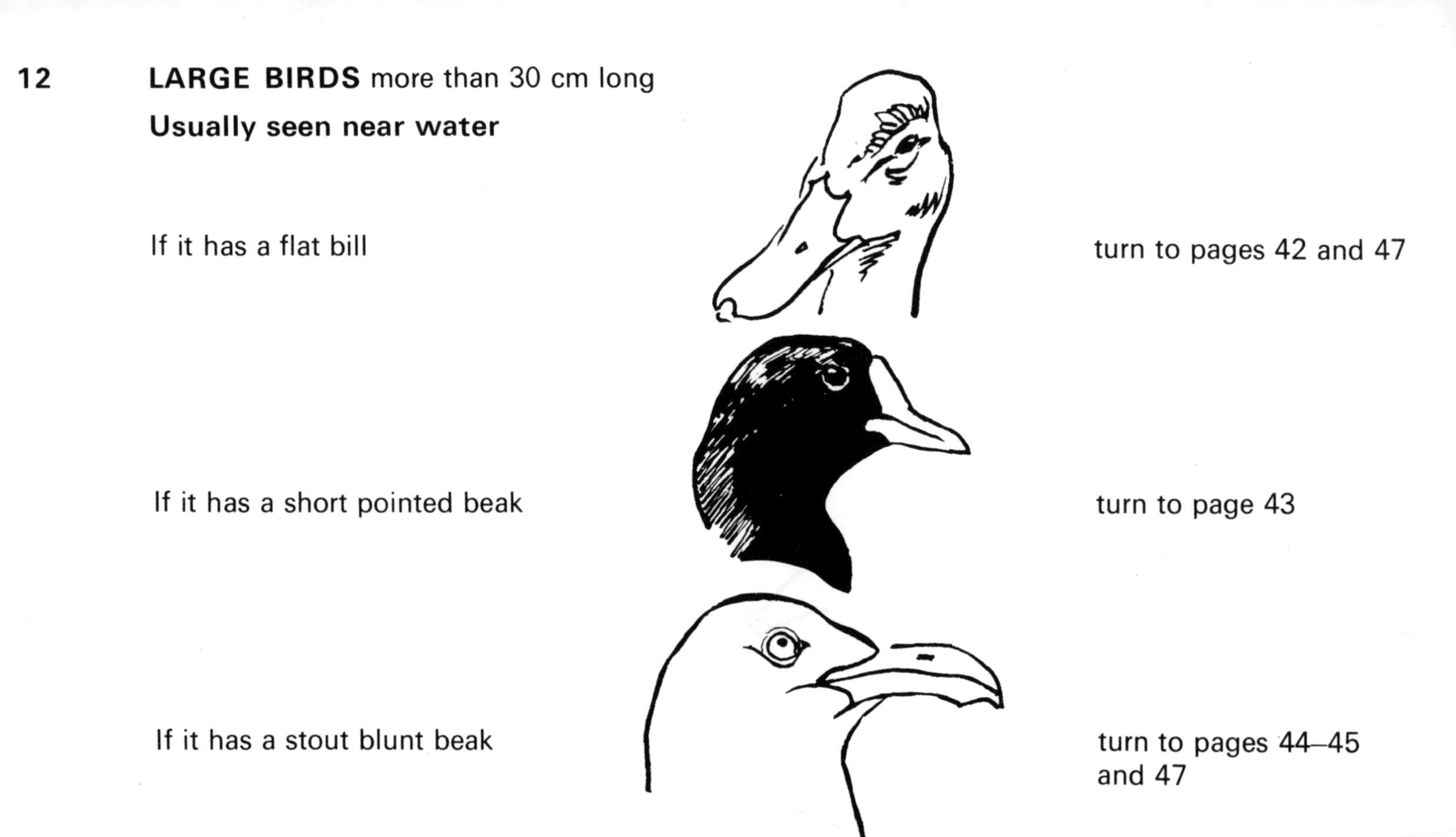

If it has a flat bill turn to pages 42 and 47

If it has a short pointed beak turn to page 43

If it has a stout blunt beak turn to pages 44–45 and 47

If it has a long pointed beak and long legs turn to pages 46–47

LARGE BIRDS more than 30 cm long

Usually seen away from water

If it has a pointed beak and crest turn to page 46

If it has a stout beak turn to pages 37, 38, 39

If it has a long strong beak turn to page 36

If it has a very short beak turn to pages 37 and 41

If it has a hooked beak turn to page 40

FEET

It is sometimes possible to find the feet of dead birds; these can be mounted and kept for closer observation.

If the foot has three toes in front and one strong toe behind and if the bird lives where there are trees and bushes, it belongs to one of the perching birds.

turn to pages 24–33
and 35
37–39

If it has two toes forwards and two behind, it belongs either to a cuckoo or a woodpecker—the outer toe can turn forwards or backwards.

turn to pages 36–37

If it has four toes pointing forwards, it belongs to a swift.

turn to page 34

If it has hooked toes, called talons, it belongs to a bird of prey.

turn to page 40

If the foot has three toes in front and one smaller toe behind and if the bird lives near water, it probably belongs to one of the wading birds or a moorhen; if on land, to a game bird or pigeon.

turn to pages 39, 41, 43
46–47

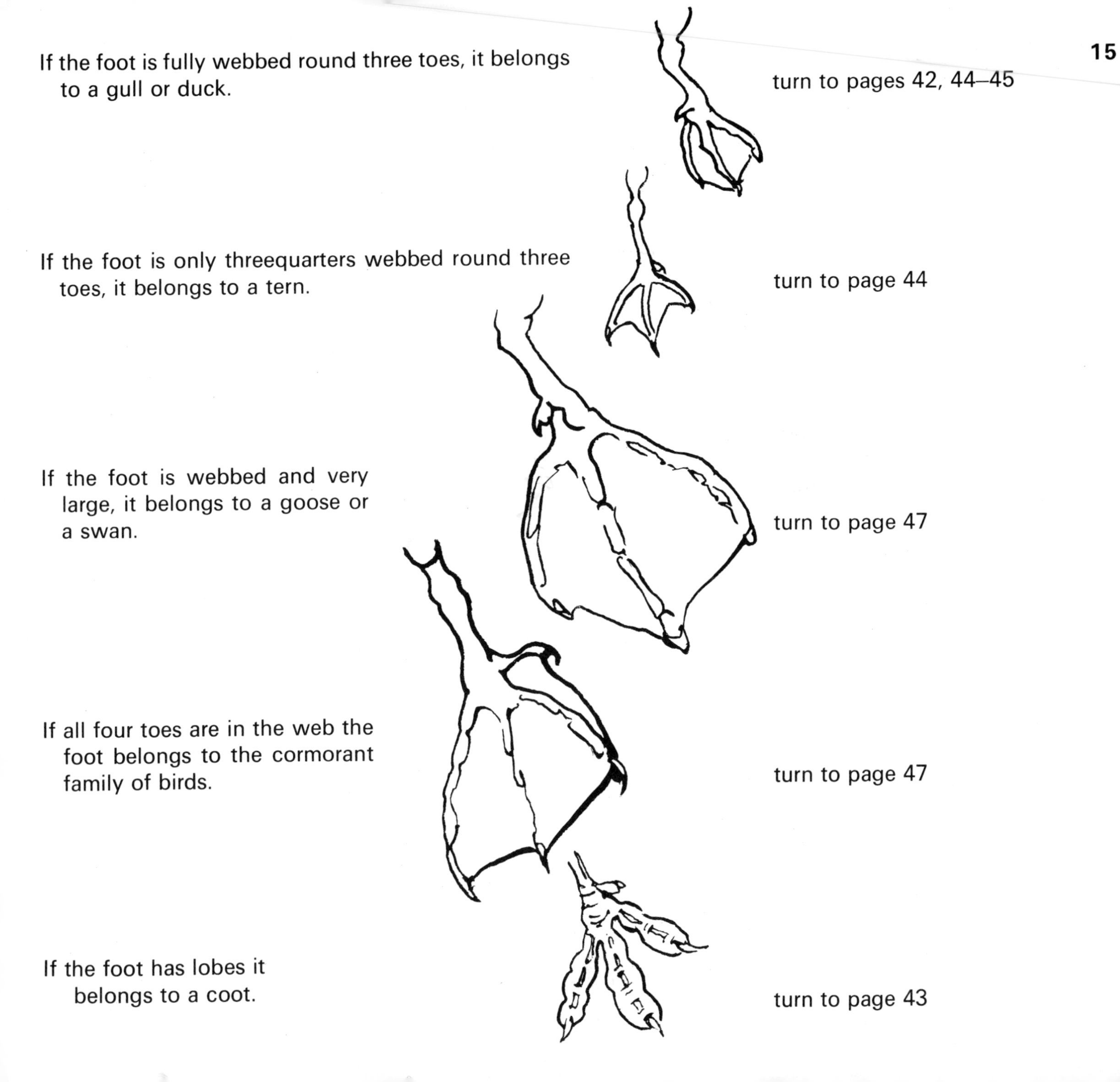

If the foot is fully webbed round three toes, it belongs to a gull or duck.

turn to pages 42, 44–45

If the foot is only threequarters webbed round three toes, it belongs to a tern.

turn to page 44

If the foot is webbed and very large, it belongs to a goose or a swan.

turn to page 47

If all four toes are in the web the foot belongs to the cormorant family of birds.

turn to page 47

If the foot has lobes it belongs to a coot.

turn to page 43

FOOTPRINTS

You may find footprints in sand, mud or snow or you can put a tray of wet sand or mud near the bird table. Measure the footprints and draw them life size in your field notebook.

If they show a long hind toe they were probably made by perching birds (pages 24–33; 35–39).
If they were arranged like this the bird was hopping.

If they were arranged like this the bird was running or walking.

If they have a short hind toe, or none, they were probably made by a wader (page 46), or a pigeon (page 39), or a game bird (page 41) or a moorhen (page 43).

If the prints are this shape they were made by a bird with a webbed foot (pages 42, 44–45, 47). There is often only a tiny prick from the hind claw.

You can make a plaster cast of a footprint

You will need:

a small tin	some plaster of Paris
a stick for stirring	water
stiff paper	paint
paper clips	clear varnish
	penknife

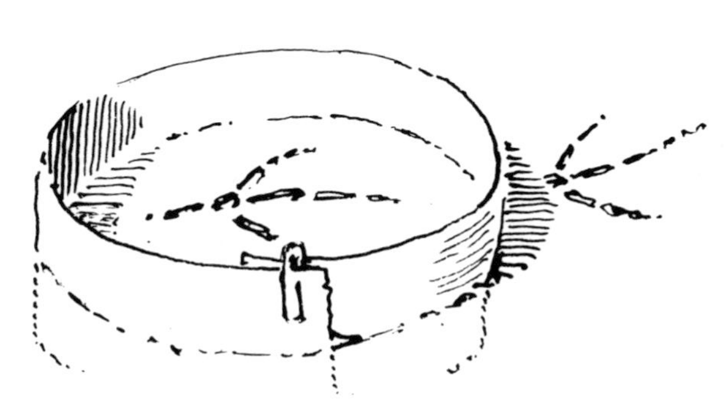

Put a strip of paper about 3 cm wide around the foot-print. Hold the ends of the strip together with a paper clip.

Decide how much water would be needed to fill the space surrounded by the paper. Put a little less than this into the tin. Add plaster a little at a time, keeping it well stirred, until the mixture is thick but can be poured into the paper ring. Pour the mixture over the footprints and make the top smooth. You will get used to the quantities when you have done this several times.

Leave it to dry until it is hard; this should take about 10 minutes.

When it is hard, remove the paper and very carefully lever up the plaster cast with a penknife. Remove any large pieces of mud.

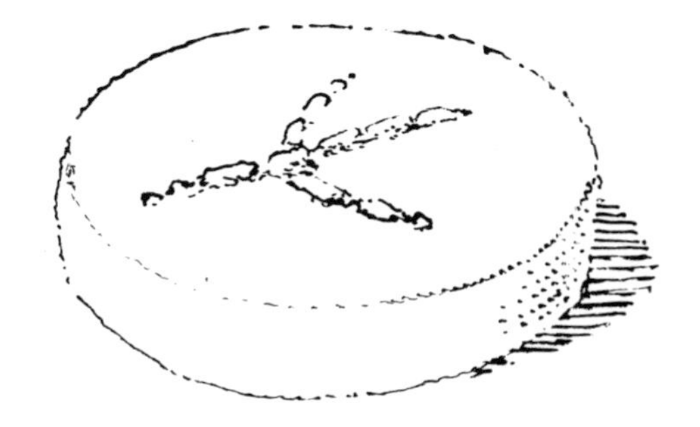

When the cast is really hard, wash off the rest of the mud with a soft nailbrush or old toothbrush.

Paint the shape of the footprint, and then varnish the whole cast with clear varnish.

BIRD SHAPES IN THE AIR dotted lines show flight paths

When you see a bird like one of these turn to the page number by it.

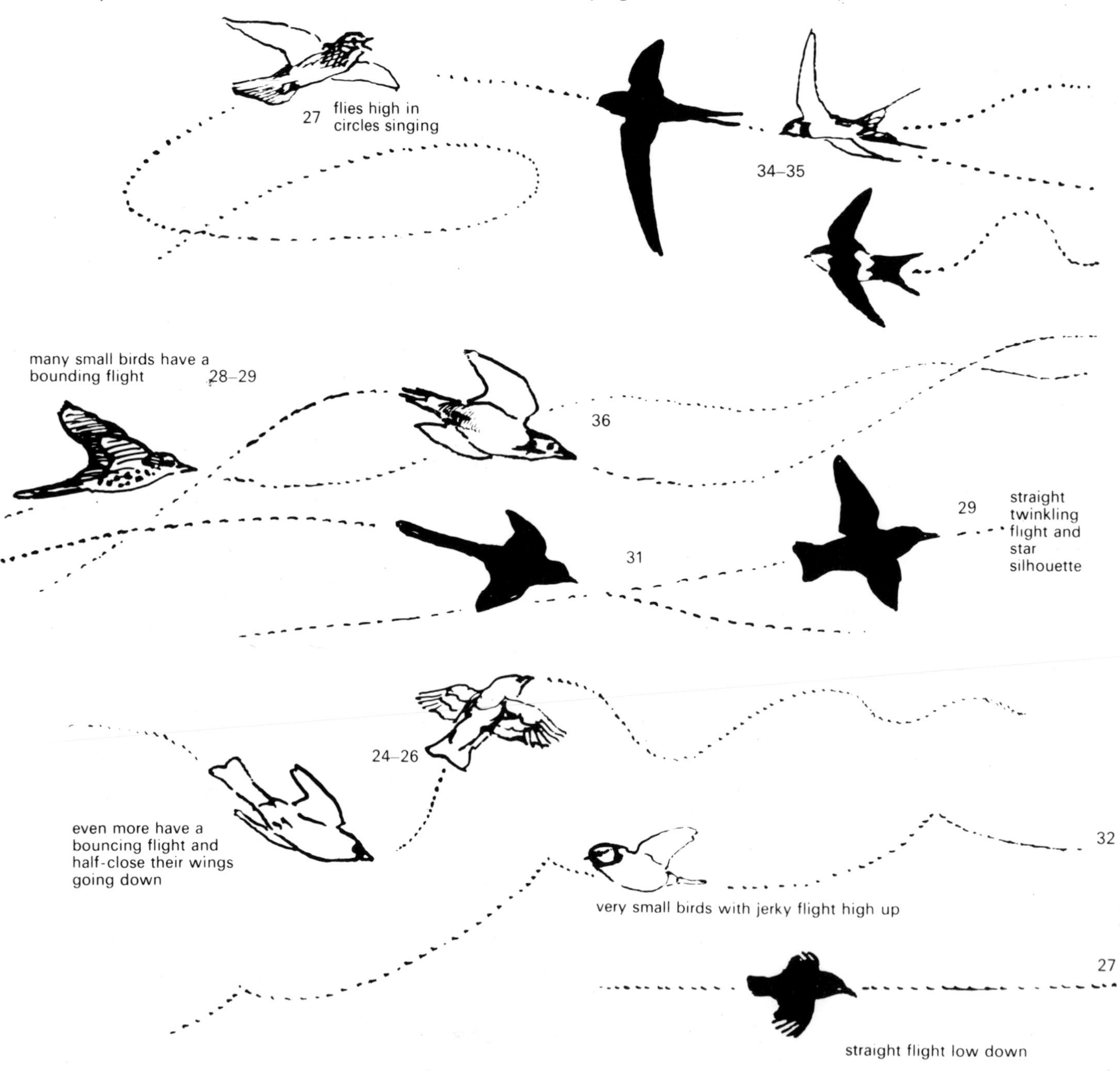

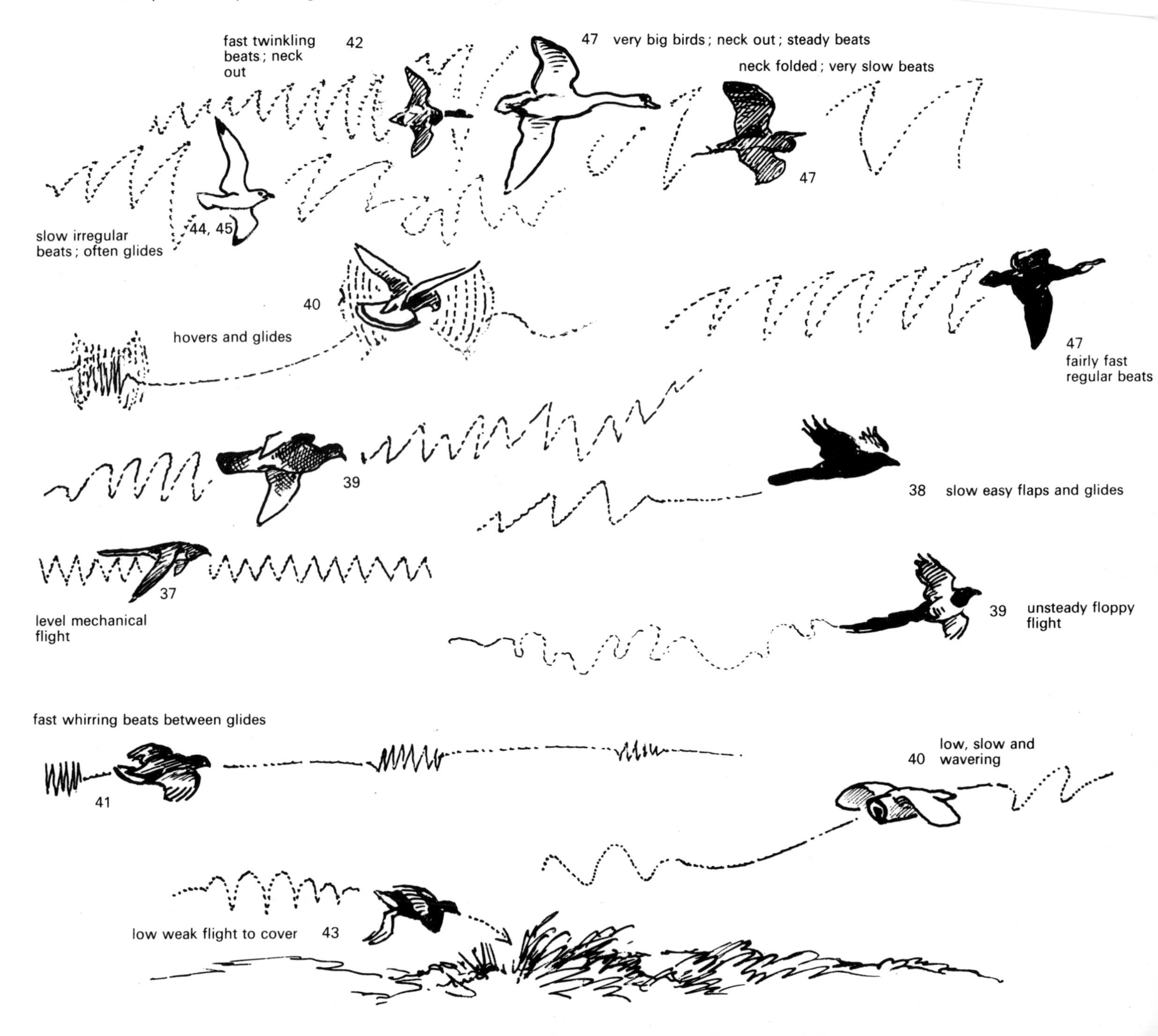
dotted lines show speed and depth of wing beats
fast twinkling beats; neck out
42
47 very big birds; neck out; steady beats
neck folded; very slow beats
47
slow irregular beats; often glides
44, 45
40
hovers and glides
47
fairly fast regular beats
39
38 slow easy flaps and glides
37
level mechanical flight
39 unsteady floppy flight
fast whirring beats between glides
41
40 low, slow and wavering
low weak flight to cover 43

BIRD SHAPES ON LAND

all these birds walk (except 26)

When you see a bird like one of these turn to the page number by it.

BIRD SHAPES IN TREES

Look for shapes, patterns, and angle they perch at

BIRD SHAPES ON THE WATER

BIRD FAMILIES

Birds that are alike in shape and which behave in the same way belong to groups called families. Ducks and geese and swans all belong to the ANATIDAE family. Thrushes and blackbirds and robins belong to the TURDIDAE family. Ornithologists (people who study birds) have made up these family names from Latin words.

In each family group are different kinds of birds, or as ornithologists say, different species. In the TURDIDAE family, the blackbird belongs to one species, the song thrush to another, and the mistle thrush to another. In the PARIDAE family the blue tit belongs to one species, the great tit to another, the coal tit to another.

The cocks and hens of some kinds of birds have plumage of different colours. Sometimes the young are different from their parents. Some birds have different coloured plumage in winter and summer.

The drawings of birds on pages 24–27 and 30–35 are drawn to their real size. The drawings of the other birds are less than their real size. The silhouettes show the size of the birds compared to the size of the house sparrow.

house sparrows

rook to same scale
as sparrows

SMALL BIRDS WITH STRONG, STUMPY BEAKS for cracking seeds

All finches have a bouncing flight (see page 18) and may be seen in hedgerows, fields and gardens. During the winter different kinds of finches fly and feed together. These collections of birds are called flocks.

Chaffinches have white feathers on their shoulders. They make smooth, felted nests of moss, roots and lichen, lined with hair. The young birds are like the hen.

Greenfinches have deep yellow feathers on wings and tail. They nest in bushes making a tidy nest of twigs, moss, wool and grass and lining it with hair. The young birds are brown and striped. The cock begins to sing in February. The most easily recognised note is rather like a creaking door.

Goldfinches have a scarlet patch on the head and yellow and black wings. The young birds have brown heads. Goldfinches may be seen fluttering among plants, hanging from fruiting heads looking for seeds, or in flocks twittering all the time. They make a small, deep nest of moss, roots and lichens and line it with wool or down.
The cock sings nearly all the year round.

Bullfinches have black crowns and white rumps. The young birds have a white rump but no black crown.
They nest in thick bushes, making a shallow nest of fine wigs, and lining it with black rootlets.
In spring bullfinches may eat the flower buds on fruit trees.

Sparrows
family Passeridae

House sparrows live in crowds: they are very quarrelsome and chirrup noisily. They nest in roofs and barns, under eaves and in ivy or creepers. Their large, untidy nests are made of straw and other odd bits and pieces and lined with wool and feathers. Sometimes they steal other birds' nests. The young birds are like the hen. Because house sparrows sometimes sleep in their nests they may be seen collecting bedding all the year round. For a short time in late summer they migrate to nearby cornfields and during the winter may be seen feeding in fields with finches.

House sparrow
cock and hen

Tree sparrow

Tree sparrows have a chocolate brown crown and black patch on the cheek.
They build the same kind of nest as the house sparrow but in holes in trees, in thatch and barns.
They are less common than the house sparrow in built up areas.

Skylarks may be seen over parks and open country soaring up into the sky singing as they fly.
They nest in shallow holes in the ground which they line with grass.

Wren *family Troglodytidae*

Skylark *family Alaudidae*

Wrens are small restless birds that move about like mice among dried leaves, low plants and bushes.
They have tiny turned-up tails. Their song, a series of trills, is surprisingly loud for so small a bird.
The domed nest, made of dried leaves and other material is lined with feathers and has a hole in the side.
It is built in low bushes, ivied trunks, or walls.

Thrushes *family Turdidae*

Song thrush

Mistle thrushes may be seen in garden and wayside trees or feeding in open country. They sing high up in the trees beginning in mid-winter and chase rivals away with rattling cries. The nest, made of dried grass and mud, is built in forked branches of trees.

Mistle thrush

Song thrushes may be seen in woods, hedges and gardens. They crack snail shells using stones as anvils. Their song is varied, each new phrase is repeated several times. The nest of grass and twigs lined with mud is built in low bushes.

Blackbirds may be seen in hedges and gardens almost everywhere. Their song is mellow and very varied; it can be heard from early spring. The alarm and good night calls are harsh notes repeated rapidly. The nest, built in bushes and on ledges, is made of twigs and mud and lined with grass. Blackbirds raise and fan their tails as they land.

An old **Starling** *family Sturnidae* with a young starling in front

A pair of **Blackbirds** *family Turdidae* the hen in front; cock behind

Starlings may be seen almost anywhere quarrelling and waddling about probing for grubs. They make whistling, clicking noises and mimic other birds' song. They nest in holes. Many starlings are resident in Britain but large flocks from Russia and Norway come to spend the winter here.

Robins
family Turdidae
young and old

Dunnocks though sparrow-like, hav
slender beaks and a slate grey breas
they also sing.
They nest in bushes near the grounc
making the nest of moss and twigs an
lining it with hair, wool and feathers.
They move jerkily among low bushes i
gardens and hedgerows.

Robins are friendly, cheeky little birds that live in gardens, hedgerows and woods.
A pair of robins claim an area of land, called a territory, as their feeding ground. After the breeding season the pair splits up and each robin has its own territory.
The nest is built near the ground in holes in banks, in hollow tree stumps, buildings, pots and baskets; it is made of moss and dead leaves and lined with hair.
The young are speckled; their red breast feathers do not appear until late summer. Their very varied, high pitched song may be heard almost all the year round.

Dunnock (or Hedge sparrow)
family Prunellidae

Pied wagtails
family Motacillidae
old and young

Pied wagtails are black and white birds that run about in parks and gardens and by water wagging their long tails ready to spring after flies.
They nest in hollow trees, niches in walls or buildings and under bridges, making the nest of moss, dead leaves and grass and lining it with hair, feathers and wool.

SMALL BIRDS WITH SMALL, SHARP BEAKS used for picking insects out of cracks

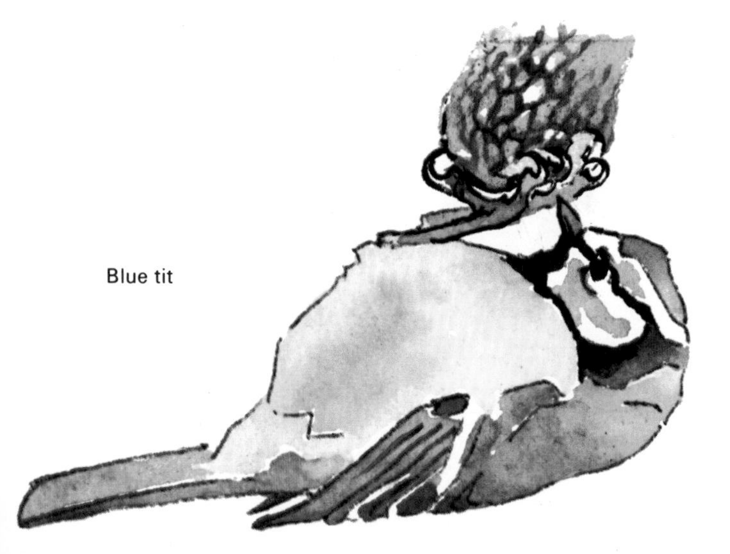

Blue tit

Great tit. The cock has bolder and shinier markings than the hen.

Tits often hang upside down or fly about jerkily in woods, hedges and gardens searching for food. In spring their quiet, short song can be heard all day long. But a loud 'Tee-cher' is the usual note of the great tit.

Blue and Great tits are frequent visitors to bird tables if there are bushes nearby.

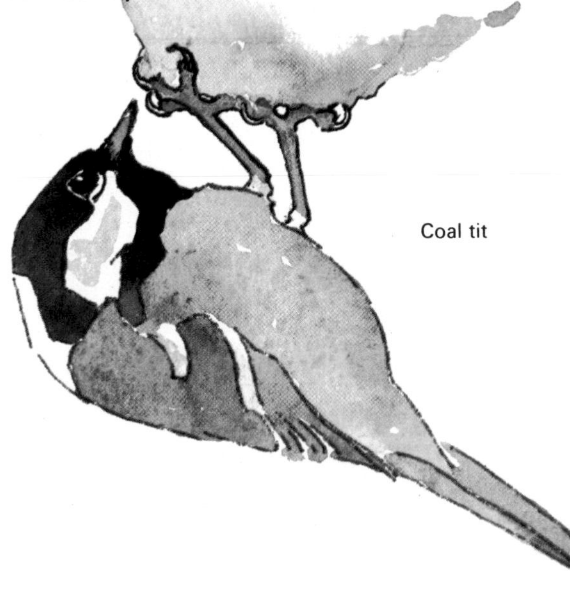

Coal tit

The **Coal tit** is often seen near conifer trees. They nest in banks, walls, tree trunks or nesting boxes, making the nest of moss and grass and lining it with hair and wool.

Long-tailed tit

Long-tailed tits live in woods and open country; they hunt restlessly along the hedgerows twittering all the time.
Their oval nests, made of moss and lichen, are lined with feathers; they have a hole in the side.

Nuthatches may be seen in gardens, parks and woodlands running jerkily up and down trees. They wedge nuts in the bark of trees and peck at them. They nest in holes in trees which they line with bark and dead leaves and plaster the entrance with mud to make it smaller.

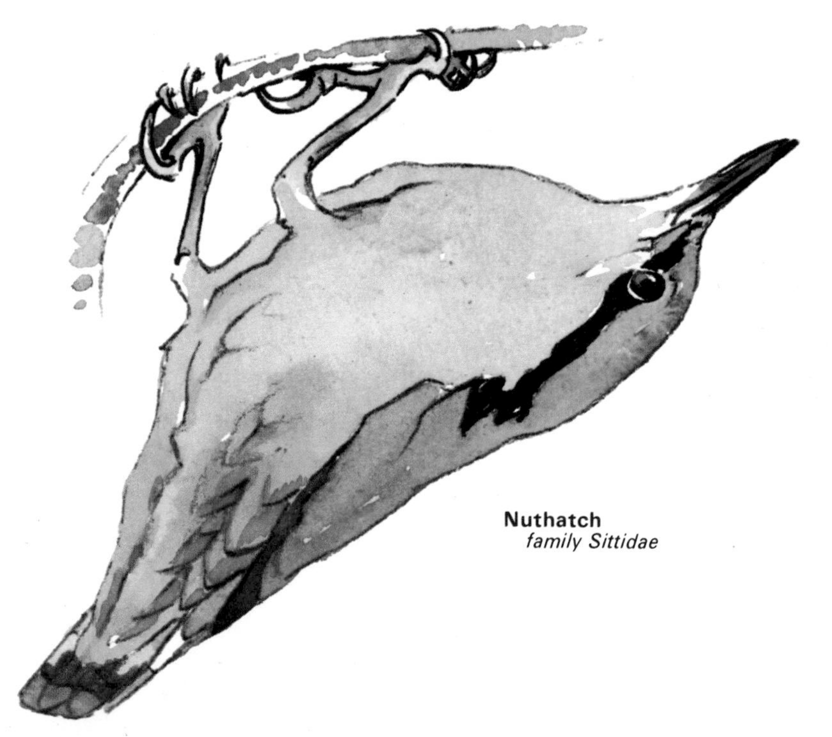

Nuthatch
family Sittidae

SMALL BIRDS WITH FORKED TAILS and a wheeling flight

Swift
family Apodidae

Swifts, Swallows and Martins come to Britain in spring. During the summer they rear their young and in the autumn they all return to their winter quarters. This movement from one place to another is called migration. Their long, slender bodies and very long pointed wings make it possible for them to swoop and wheel when catching insects in their gaping mouths.

Swifts are blacker and larger than swallows and martins. Because they have weak legs they cannot walk on the ground and can only take off from high places. They cling to walls and cliffs with their forward pointing toes. They often fly together around roof tops and high buildings screeching as they go and spend the night high up in the air. They nest in tall buildings or in cracks on cliffs.

House martins have white rumps and white underparts and shorter tails than swallows.
They build their nests on walls under the eaves of houses and barns using mud mixed with saliva and dried grass. The nests have a small hole at the top and are lined with wool and feathers. When in their nests they twitter continuously.
Flocks of both martins and swallows sit on telegraph wires and roof tops especially before migration.

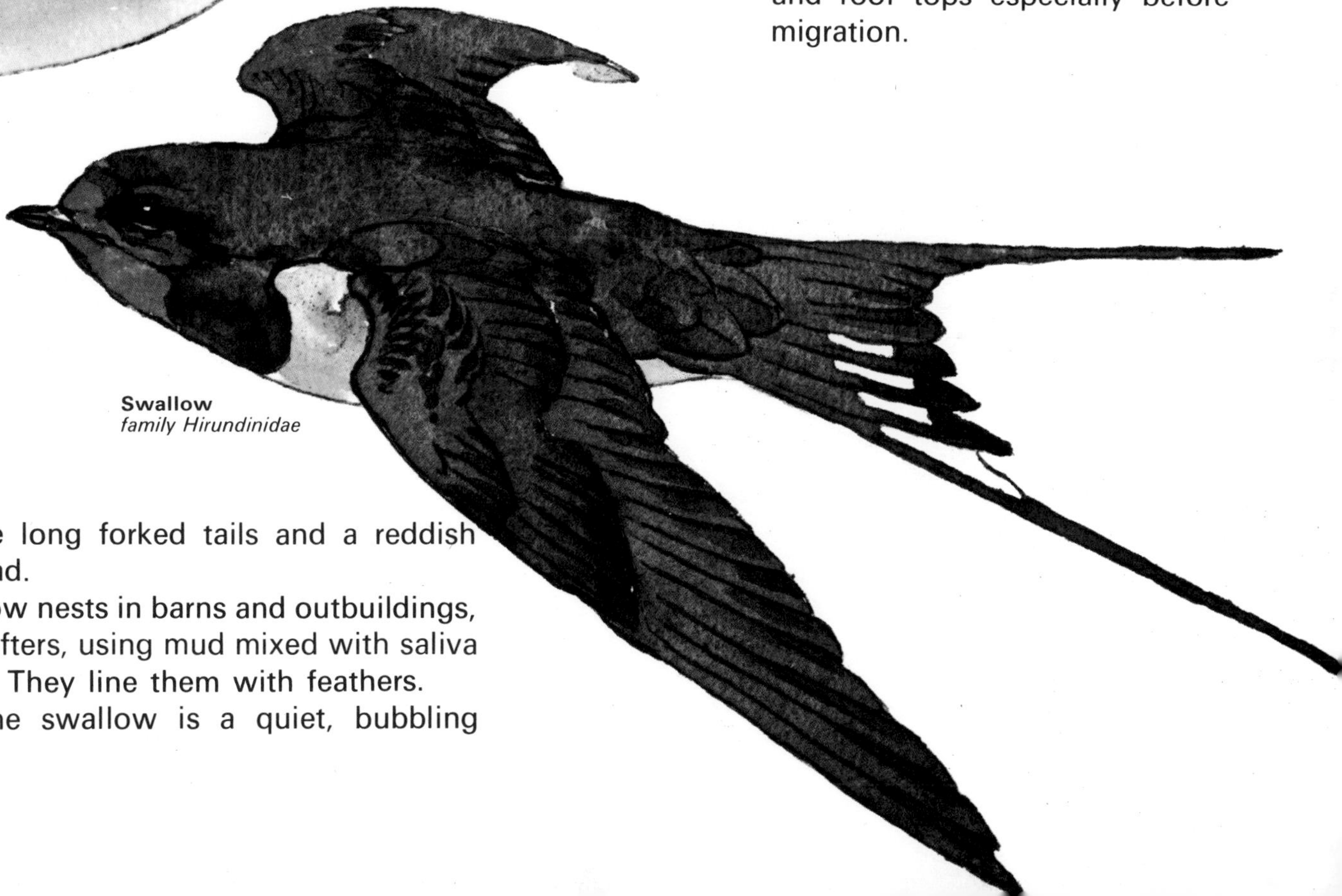

House martin
family Hirundinidae

Swallow
family Hirundinidae

Swallows have long forked tails and a reddish patch on the head.
They build shallow nests in barns and outbuildings, on ledges and rafters, using mud mixed with saliva and dried grass. They line them with feathers.
The song of the swallow is a quiet, bubbling twitter.

Woodpeckers live in parks and woodlands. Using their beaks they chisel out holes in old tree trunks. They drum loudly in spring. They nest in the holes: the eggs are laid about a foot below the entrance, no nesting material is used. With their long, sticky tongues they catch insects from the trunks of trees using their short tails and feet with two toes in front and two behind, to support themselves.

Woodpeckers
family Picidae

Spotted woodpeckers

The pair of **Spotted woodpeckers** are at the nest hole; the hen has no red on its head. They rarely feed on the ground, but may come to the bird table for nuts and fat.

Green woodpeckers may be seen on the ground digging for ants: because they have a loud laughing call note they are called 'Yaffles'.

Cuckoos arrive from southern Europe in April when the well known song of the male bird and the long bubbling sound of the hen may be heard. They fly over wooded areas. The hens lay eggs in smaller birds' nests. The young cuckoo throws out the other young birds and is fed by the foster parents. Old cuckoos fly away in July; the young go later.

Cuckoo *family Cuculidae*

Jays are shy woodland birds but often visit gardens to steal fruit, peas and beans; they rob nests. Jays have a harsh shrieking cry and are more often heard than seen. They build their nests of twigs in the undergrowth or in trees and line them with fine roots, hair or wool.

Jay *family Corvidae*

Rooks nest in tree top colonies where they caw noisily in the spring. They may be seen flying about in flocks. Old rooks have bare white faces; young rooks' faces are black, their plumage is iridescent.

Crows are useful scavengers as they feed on dead animals; they also eat worms, grubs and corn. They all build stick nests.

Crows *family Corvidae*

Jackdaws may be seen feeding with rooks; they can be recognised by their grey napes and smaller size. They build their nests in holes in trees or old buildings.

Rook

Jackdaw

Carrion crow

Carrion crows may be seen flying about alone or in pairs. They are less noisy than jackdaws or rooks but often repeat their harsh caws three times. Their plumage is tidier than that of the rooks.

Magpie *family Corvidae*

Magpies may be seen, usually in pairs, in wooded parks or on farmland and heard chattering noisily in trees. They build a big nest with a thorny dome in trees or tall bushes. They are most easily recognised by their black and white plumage and very long tail.

Wood pigeons live in trees and fly out to feed in open country. A few may be seen in parks and squares among the town pigeons; they are easily recognised by their white neck rings and wing patches. They are sometimes called Ring doves. When displaying they fly up and down clapping their wings together. Pigeons feed greedily on corn, seeds and fruits; in gardens they strip peas, beans and cabbages. They build their nests in trees using only a few sticks. The young, called squabs, are fed on 'pigeon's milk' which they take from the mouths of the parent birds.

Wood pigeon *family Columbidae*

LARGE BIRDS WITH HOOKED BEAKS CALLED BIRDS OF PREY

Owls hunt at night and may be heard calling to each other as they fly. Their soft plumage gives them silent flight which helps them when hunting for small mammals, birds and insects. After feeding, owls bring up pellets made of the hard cases, bones and fur of the animals they have eaten.

Tawny owls hoot 'Tu-whit, tu-whoo'.
Barn owls are a much paler brown with white faces; they have a wild shrieking call.
Little owls repeat a single low whistle.

Hawks hunt during the day and may be seen soaring high up in the sky or swooping down on animals they see below. The one most often seen is the kestrel. After feeding hawks also bring up pellets.

Owls and kestrels lay their eggs in hollow trees or in old crows' or magpies' nests.

Tawny owl

Little owl

Cock kestrel

Owls
family Strigidae

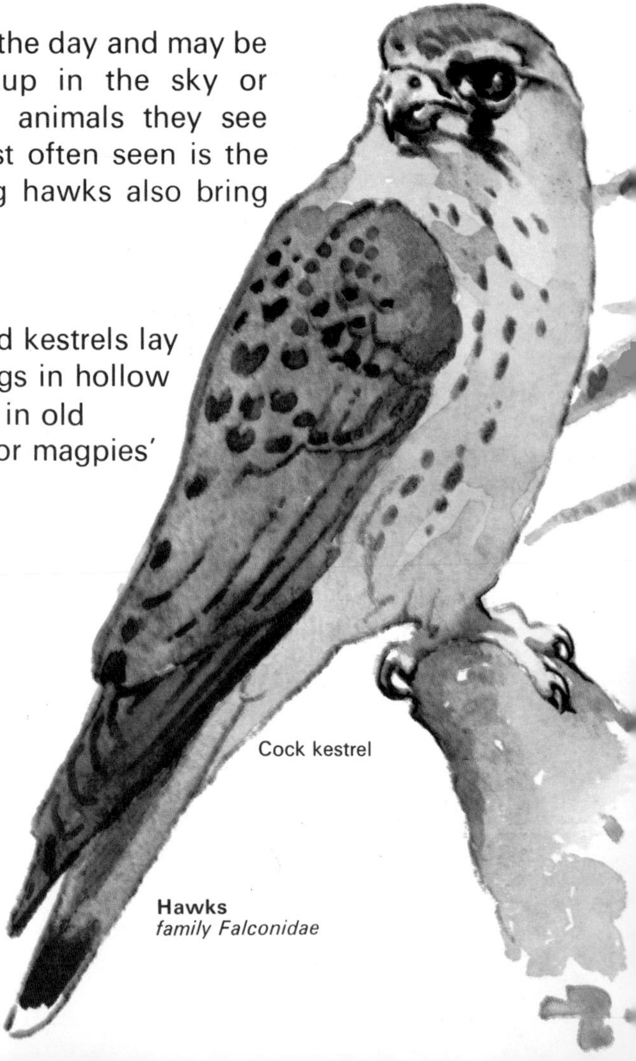

Hawks
family Falconidae

Pheasants and **Partridges** have strong feet like fowls for scratching up ants, beetles, bulbs and seeds. Their short rounded wings help them to rise quickly into the air. They fly noisily, but not far; they more often run when disturbed. The eggs are laid in hollows scratched in the ground among bushes or long grass and lined with a few dead leaves.

Pheasants
family Phasianidae

Hen pheasant

Cock pheasant

Partridge

The eggs are covered with grass and leaves until a full clutch of about twenty eggs is laid. The downy chicks are able to run about as soon as they hatch. In order to lure enemies away from their young, parent birds may pretend to have a broken wing.
They are called game birds because they are shot for sport.

LARGE BIRDS WITH FLAT BILLS
living near water

Ducks *family Anatidae*

Mallard
duck, drake and duckling

Flocks of ducks may be seen on rivers and lakes. Their webbed feet help them to swim, and they have fleshy fringes round their bills for sifting small animals and plants from the water.

Nests of grass and leaves, lined with down, are built in the undergrowth. The ducklings can swim as soon as they hatch. In late summer the drakes are in eclipse; they lose their brightly coloured feathers and become like dark ducks.

Mallards dabble and up-end in shallow water looking for food.

Tufted ducks have a drooping tuft of feathers behind their heads, they dive for food.

Tufted drake
with its tiny dark
duckling behind it

Moorhens and **Coots** live on lakes and rivers in both town and country. They build large nests among reeds and rushes: the chicks swim as soon as they hatch. Both coot and moorhen jerk their heads up and down as they swim; they feed on water plants and small animals. Moorhens jerk their black and white tails as they walk about near the rushes or run over floating water weeds, helped by their long spreading toes. Young moorhens are browner and paler than their parents.

Moorhens

Moorhen and **Coot** *family Rallidae*

Coots have curious lobed feet (see page 15) but no visible tail. They swim and dive in open water. The black, fluffy chicks have red haloes: they swim around cheeping noisily while their parents dive for food. Young coots have white breasts.

Coots

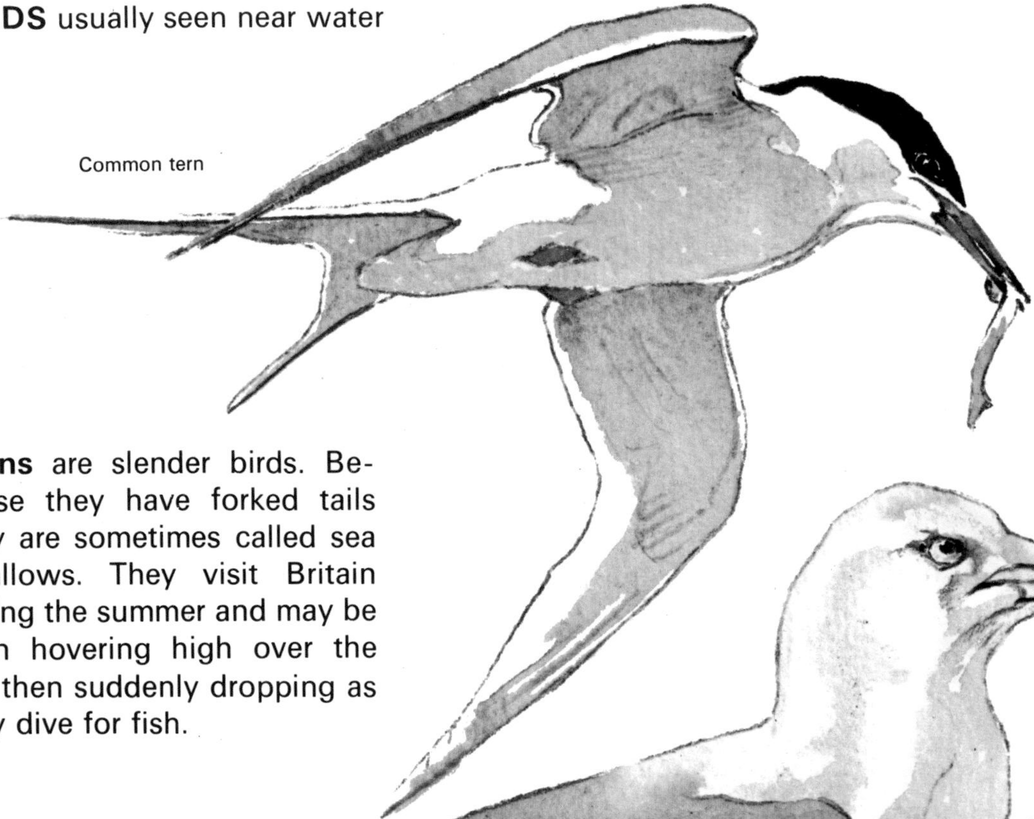

Common tern

Gulls *family Laridae*

Terns are slender birds. Because they have forked tails they are sometimes called sea swallows. They visit Britain during the summer and may be seen hovering high over the sea then suddenly dropping as they dive for fish.

Gulls may be seen near the sea, on rivers and lakes or in open country. Their long slender wings help them to wheel, swoop and soar and to fly long distances between their feeding and roosting places. Gulls are greedy feeders; they eat small sea and land animals and also scavenge. They build bulky nests on the ground using dry plants that grow near the nesting site. The chicks are fluffy and run about as soon as they hatch.

Herring gull

b. in its breeding plumage (January–June)

Black headed gull

. in its winter plumage (July–December) without its dark head

c. a young gull in its juvenile plumage (May–October)

l young gulls have mott-
d brown and white plum-
ge in their first year. In the
cond year most gulls are
e their parents but have
black band on their tail.
ne herring gull takes five
ars to change from juve-
le to adult plumage.
ne colours of their beaks
d feet help to distin-
uish different kinds of
lls.

Common gull

LARGE BIRDS WITH POINTED BEAKS AND LONG LEGS

Waders are usually seen in the shallow water of bays and estuaries, running about and digging out small animals with their long pointed beaks.

The nests are built on the ground; the chicks are fluffy and run about as soon as they hatch.

Many waders go north to breed, some beyond the Arctic circle.

Some waders have different summer and winter plumage.

If the wader you see is not shown here look in other bird books to find its name.

Lapwings are wading birds but are more often seen inland. They have short beaks and are easily recognised by the crest on their heads. Because of the sound of their cry they are often called Peewits.

usually seen near water

wan *family Anatidae*

Cormorant *family Phalacrocoracidae*

Cormorants are usually seen, with their wings outspread, on rocks at sea.

Canada Goose *family Anatidae*

Herons stand in shallow water looking for food. They nest in high trees in colonies.

/**ild geese** of many different kinds and swans ay be seen on large estuaries and marshland ear the sea. Many geese only visit Britain in inter.

anada geese may often be seen grazing in arks.

Heron *family Ardeidae*

These big birds are not drawn to the same scale as the waders

Index

Bibliography

Allen, Gwen, and Denslow, Joan, *Bones* (O.U.P. 1968).
Bosiger, E., and Guilcher, J. M., *A Bird is Born* (Oliver & Boyd, 1960).
Conder, Peter, *British Garden Birds*, including records of bird song (Record Books Ltd, and Royal Society for the Protection of Birds, 1966).
Ennion, E. A. R., *Bird Study in a Garden* (Puffin Picture Book, 1958).
Fisher, James, *The Migration of Birds* (Bodley Head, 1966).
Fitter, R. S. R., and Richardson, R. A., *The Pocket Guide to Nests and Eggs* (Collins, 1954).
Hutchinson, M. M., *A Bird Table* (Making and Keeping Series. Ward Lock, 1957).
Peterson, R., Mountfort, G., and Hollom, P. A. D., *A Field Guide to the Birds of Britain and Europe* (Collins, 1954).
Tunnicliffe, C. F., *Birds of the Estuary* (Puffin Picture Book).